I0162672

The Suicide Cafe

Michael Bryson

Inner Core of Rage Press

Copyright © 2019 Michael Bryson

ISBN: 978-0-578-22644-6

Table of Contents

Preface

These poems, verse and prose, were written over a series of years in which illusions were slowly falling away, while the contours of a never-entirely-welcoming reality were coming more clearly into focus. It may be that every life is a Pyrrhic struggle, with occasional (if costly) victories, but the losses inevitably mount, and must be faced in time. These lines are about those losses. I would never claim to be a poet—a mantle often too-lightly worn by those, like me, whom it does not truly fit—so perhaps I should not describe what is written here as poetry. Still, these lines have something to say of self- and other-discovery, describing the final stages of a journey from hope to acceptance.

—Michael Bryson

The Suicide Cafe

The special for today is Hemingway,
though Plath and Sexton are quite good as well;
Virginia Woolf is popular, of course,
if somewhat overdone, and *so* last year.

Perhaps Empedocles is more your style?
for those who'd like to go out with a bang,
volcanic lava really can't be beat,
and nicely solves the problem of remains.

If this is somewhat garish for your taste,
the artist in the garret might well serve;
a Thomas Chatterton, unrecognized
by editors and hacks, in poison's arms.

But save some room to taste a sweet or two,
Mishima's blade will surely cut the fat.

The Awful Rowing (for Anne Sexton)

The awful rowing goes on, day by day,
but not toward God, or something in the place
of God; despite the shorter breath of days
through which we manage to survive once more,

the rowing aims at nothing in the end,
no final destination gives it point
or meaning; still, the muscles ache with strain,
and sweat pours down our faces with each stroke

of oars in water leading to no shore,
no resting place in sight, unless we see
an end worth calling by that name in death,
a shaping principle to aimless tales.

But death knows nothing more, no secret stores
of wisdom give this awful rowing shape.

State of the Art

We write our poems with a studied air
too casual to be indifferent, yet
somehow about such things as grapefruit rinds,
and all the ways their bitter pith sums up

relationships, both modeled and engaged,
the disappointments that we revel in
while tossing new-read pages to the floor,
the mic drop of the newly-vegan rockstar

too frail for irony, whose coiling words
require more than unreflective strength,
but cannot find the source to fuel their wit
aside from borrowed phrases, attitudes,

a certain flippancy in place of craft,
and prose, disguised by random breaks, as verse.

Muse, Beyond a Blind Man's Reach

I would but serve her, with my pen-sketched lines,
the words with which I reach for her at night,
yet she will not acknowledge me by day,
denies she knows me, keeps me wrapped in dark,
a secret she relies on me to keep,
and so I do, because a fool knows naught
but how to play the games of foolishness,
to listen to the heartfelt promises
that someday she will be with me, if time
and silence have their way, if I will wait,
and let another year go by (which store
of years begins to seem exhaustible,
where once they well appeared as endless days),
and if her plans succeed, and all goes well,
and nothing intervenes or interferes,
and I am nothing like the kind of fool
who would insist on being recognized
and not deny the hopes I let myself
drag once again into the harshest light
of day, where all my faults will be exposed,
my failures and my flaws, the ugly stains
of lived experience that will not out
no matter how I wash, and wash again...

Then someday she will visit me, perhaps,
and she will take me out into the light,
without the need to feel ashamed of me,
or keep me wrapped in silent secrecy,
so I will once again know what it is
to write of love, and have it be the truth.

The Stranger

Which one among you is the stranger here?
Whose eyes see through the skin we hide behind,
pretending we are men of parts whose words
might stand for truth before a wretched world
whose plotline always leads to tragic ends,
though played by actors who cannot rehearse
forgotten lines for never-written roles
whose audience is blind, insensible,
and dumb beyond the hope of miracles.

Which one among you has the tragic flaw,
intelligence too great to fit the plot
you find yourself condemned once more to play?
Your entrances and exits never change,
and brilliance cannot save you on the stage
where old conventions must be served each night:
revenge, the comedy of lovers, fools,
the grasping kings whose wars, in honor's name,
leave countless Hotspurs bleeding in the dust
they turn to mud with drops of red-tinged life,
returning to the nothing whence they came.

Which one among you has the curse of sight,
and walks alone amidst the eyeless crowds?

Unnoticed (for Charles Bukowski)

Some suicides are never recorded,
the slow descents, the acquiescences,
the disappointed men who quietly
submit their necks to power's crushing yoke,

and feel themselves grow smaller by the day
while all their dreams lie fallow, indistinct,
revealed for what they always were, the frauds
of youth, the fantasies they soon would learn

to compromise, for life consumes their eyes,
leaves husks in place of men, with no more room
for love or play, for possibilities
now circumscribed by choices made in haste.

Such deaths remain unnoticed by the crowds
of dead who fill our mirrors and our streets.

The Troubadour in Winter

When bright magnolia blossoms first appear
before the dying winter takes revenge
with rough winds tearing buds that scatter down
amongst unfinished cigarettes and trash,

the condom wrappers lying in the mud,
mute witnesses to pilgrims' desperate pleas
for love, or something writhing in its place
in pain or ecstasy, still intertwined,

I think of all my foolishness and hope,
and hate myself for my belief in lies,
the promises of youth, the simple gods

of Bronze-age fairy tales, whose rights and wrongs
were always lighter than the thinning air
of syllables composing ancient names

whose meanings, urgent once, are now obscure,
occult and hidden from my sense like love,
and all the promises I once believed

from those who loved, and from myself in love,
the faithfulness that each voice swears to each
while speaking sonnets from their widened eyes,

unfinished poetry whose lines drift down
amidst the fallen petals, never read,
and swept away by winter's dying winds.

Perhaps Not Yet

I cannot say exactly why I love,
since love has always come at such a cost
that I could never pay without the loss
of blood or dignity—the hurtful words

that always mark our disappointing ends,
once being called her soul-mate as she left,
while foolishly I helped her carry bags
too heavy for her as she said goodbye—

I carry weight for those I know will leave,
or play the fool, pretending I am more
than second choice (or third or fourth), and wait
for those who are not with me—*never me*—

but always somewhere else, with someone else,
and spend my nights alone, while listening
to all the sounds of life and joy outside
as couples walk, and laugh, and live a life

that I imagined once could still be mine,
but that was long ago, a dream or two
has passed into the falling mist since then,
and I have grown a wiser, sadder man

who knows he is not shaped for sportive tricks,
though not a villain yet, perhaps not yet.

Becoming Masks

The price of living under tyranny,
the lies we tell to give us space to breathe
when those who "love" us seek to curb our will
and make us like themselves, their images

of fear and hate for what they do not know
and cannot understand, a different world
whose pleasures they regard as dangerous,
whose joys resemble all the "sins" they learned

to crave and cravenly reject in youth
spent listening to those who did not know
the world they taught their children to disdain
while clinging to the ancient ways of death.

The lies grow deep, and scar us over time,
becoming masks we cannot soon remove.

Graduation Day

Just days before, I had read the letters,
the testimonials to my work by people I respect,
people whose names matter, whose work matters—
and I felt like they could not possibly be about me.
But they are. I *am* the figure they describe.
I've achieved everything I had once told myself I would,
without ever really believing my own words.
I've actually done it.

But standing here, alone
in the middle of a room of happy people,
amongst people celebrating themselves and each other,
it doesn't matter.
They all have someone, these celebrants,
someone here to laugh with,
someone to talk to,
someone to sit or stand next to.
I'm the one in the corner, nursing a cup of coffee,
then a glass of wine,
to have something to do with his hands,
to appear less awkward, less isolated, less out of place.
It doesn't work—it never really does—
and as soon as the ceremony is over,
I slip quietly out the side door.
No one sees me go.
No one notices that I am gone.

Human contact comes easily to them, it seems.
They all have someone,

friends, husbands, wives, boyfriends and girlfriends,
people who love them,
people who love them openly.
I would trade all my accomplishments to be one of them.

I will never be one of them.

A Trail of Ambiguous Picture Postcards

A poem should be long, like pain of childbirth
with penciled epidurals serving in the place of art,
otherwise, what would be the point of writing all this
prose
we cleverly disguise as verse by randomly breaking
lines without regard to rhyme or reason(less) forms
which only prove my point above—
a poem should stretch out,
allow itself the room to wind from line to line
while never quite bothering to make a point,
or do much at all
except luxuriate in its own reflected vanity,
howling in wastelands that really are nothing more
than a pale imitation, the burden of the park
on a Sunday morning, calling to the ephebes
of a long-parched imagination while making notes
toward a merely ordinary fiction, nothing elevated
enough to be called supreme—
and though we went down to the sea in ships
and assumed each what the other assumed, we
nonetheless
could not escape our derivations and borrowings,
and so we theorized
the death of bourgeois notions of originality,
positing the end of discrete (or discreet) authors,
the Romantic progenitors of our myths of origin,
and the mind-forged manacles of our despair.

Images and references and metaphors, none of them

ever quite developed or honed into anything like sense,
but left in an evocative fog of unfinished language,
dragging themselves through the unread streets
in the empty city afternoons,
while ceaselessly being borne, not into the past,
but into a time that never was nor will ever be...
and what else can we ask of our poets now,
but to reflect our own disinterest in ourselves,
to be themselves confused, uninteresting,
and lacking anything like form or function,
spark or fire, April or cruelty?

Margins

The margins of your time, the second best,
like Shakespeare's bed, bequeathed by testament
to one he saw but rarely, loved still less
than hours upon the stage and spoken words

whose meter spoke of him, but not of her,
the one he left alone each weekend night
with none to raise a glass, or share the bed,
whose real estate, just like the Stratford house,

grew far too large for one to solace in,
or serve as aught but cruel remembrances
of promises he never made to her,
just like the ones you never made to me.

I know, too well, what margins may contain,
and sleep alone, while you love somewhere else.

The Adversary

I have known madness like yours, quiet storms
just waiting to explode in wrath and rain
and blame their hailstones on the earth beneath,
always ready explanations for why

destruction is deserved, like plastic Baals
whose self-regard reveals itself in fire,
in thunder and the cries of those who die
while pelted down beneath the love of gods

who hear no other voices but their own,
so will not hear the cries of pain and fear
their wrath calls forth, unless they hear and smile,
well pleased by terror and the smell of death.

And you would have my worship out of love?
Non serviam—no matter what the cost.

Azazel

We are most alive when doing evil,
when deftly wielding daggers that appear
before our eyes, ambition and revenge
both meeting in the blade and in our hearts,

remembering the wounds we have received,
while letting slip the ones we gave to those
we claimed to love, as if we had the trick
of truly loving any but ourselves.

But yours will be the wounds I most intend,
will plan before inflicting, and enjoy
your agonies, embarrassments, and fears,
the judgments you will suffer at my hands.

The reckoning for sin is not delayed,
and you will not escape the cry of blood.

To Nobody

They're catching up, those lies you've told. Not yet,
today, next week, but all too soon enough.
You're good, perhaps the best I've ever seen.
How many people are you now? Four? Five?
All perfectly convincing, with detail
and subtle nuance, strengths and weaknesses,
even eccentricities, just as if
all of you were real. But time, that's the thing
you can't manage. You've never mastered the trick
of being here and being there at once,
and wouldn't that be a gift from the gods?
To never have to lie with words again...
When they find out, with all your masks removed,
what will you do then? Who will you be then?
Nobody? Or the braggart Greek who used
Nobody as a dangerous disguise?
Perhaps you'll take Iago's silent tack,
abandon words and never speak again.

Or maybe you'll maintain this act for years,
far longer than I think, and figure out
just how to be all things to all of us,
while never being so particular
as to insist on being anyone
at all, an actor never taking bows,
whose life's performance never ends, who struts
and frets entire lifetimes on the stage,
but all in character, while on the mark,
delivering expected lines with skill
and practiced ease. Is that your victory?

The Green Children

Upon a time in old King Stephen's reign,
in Woolpit town appeared a boy and girl
whose skin and eyes were both the purest green;
they spoke in tongues that no one understood
and ate, when they would eat, but fresh green beans.
the boy was sick, and faded soon to death,
but she remained, and learned the native ways,
soon lost her color and became a girl
that all the village men would seek unto
at night for pleasures they denied by day,
and so her wanton reputation grew
and spread the story of her magic charms.

"St. Martin's Land beneath the fields is home,
where these your foolish laws are laughed to scorn,"
said she, as those who heard her story swore,
"for there is constant twilight, never dimmed,
and joy for life that cannot be restrained.
If I could find my way, I would return,
for this too-sunlit world is made of lies
that pose as truth, and laws that would deny
the joys of life for hypocrites' mere spite."

In time, they were forgotten, swept beneath
the years, these children who would have men live
as if the moments counted as they passed.
But what of that? We have too much of truth.
Forgetting oft is best, when faced with tales
that call to us to rend illusion's veils.

Soliloquy

The sunlight doesn't always reach the dark forbidding places where we live, though by our smiles we seem to say it does—our smiles, as false today as when we first discovered how to wear them to deceive, and pose as anything but who and what we are.

Too cynical, perhaps?

Should not one look more kindly on, as men who hate their wives die cell by cell in bottles never left alone, as mothers kill their children step by step with guilt and god and sex abuse of which one mustn't speak, as children wish and pray for vengeance that will never come, while leaving bloodstains witnessing to what will never be acknowledged?

Not cynical enough?

"Love your neighbor as yourself"—why? Your neighbor is perverse—almost as much as you—and would as soon step back and let the flames engulf the world as you would, were the tables turned. And that, perhaps, is as it should be here in darkness where the sunlight cannot reach, nor ever quite illumine with reflected beams the shadows where we live, and all the darkest places where we smile, pretending to ourselves that others do not see us as we are.

So which conclusion shall we use as exculpation? Do we deceive, or are we blinded by pretense, deceiving no one but ourselves?

Does it really matter?

Imposters

Some people spend tremendous energy
on fitting in, appearing like the rest,
observing interactions, taking note
where others take for granted, practicing

what others, naturally inclined, can do
without the pains of thought, acquired skills
of presentation, necessary shows
for those without the instincts of the herd

in which they find themselves, against which rule
their measurements have always fallen short
as lacking scent, or sight, or other marks
by which the world identifies its own.

But soon enough, such secrets are exposed,
imposters in the healthy ranks cast out.

Maledictis

Insanity will always have its charms
for those of us too broken to conceal
the cracks beneath the masks we've learned to wear,
pretending all is well before we die.

But normalcy cannot disguise the wounds,
the open sores we irrigate with wine,
sedations we apply to old desires
whose painful ministrations we deny

inside the lasting hatreds of our lives,
the only things that ever truly last,
that set upon us like the ecstasies
of final days beneath the fading sun.

And so we wait, pretending to be sane,
though all the while we cannot hold a thought.

The Artist, In Blood

Each passing day brings accidental joys,
a stenciled image on a building's side,
the abstract painting hanging just inside
my line of sight while walking by at dawn,

the feel of flesh beneath my pointed blade,
still whole before the breach and rush of blood
now gushing forth to greet the buxom air
in ruddy streams whose rivulets run quick

as waterfalls that disappear in mist
on canvases that broil like Turner scenes
where paint runs thick with pain, and passions spent
with bloody fingers finishing their work.

For art must feel as bodies feel, as life
comes flowing forth still aching for release.

Through a Glass

Surprise becomes routine, illusions fade,
and all too soon we realize the truth
is not what we had hoped, no kindred souls
nor recognition's silent glance will come,

but solitude, a whisper's ancient breath
still speaking of the times before our time
when no companions walked beside their lords
and none but gods enjoyed the evening's breeze.

Those close enough to see behind our masks
will grow to have contempt for what they find
and will be right, perhaps, for what we are
is but a story much too often told.

And yet, we hope to see as we are seen,
though through a glass, to know as we are known.

Oysters

"The time has come to talk of many things,"
but menu items never understand
how soon they are to die, nor on whose teeth
will it occur to them they'll meet their end,

not overwhelmed, of course, with over-sauced,
and garish preparations, seasonal
is best, and simple, let the flavors speak
to what they were in life, now freshly killed

amidst the delicate and fragrant plates
arranged to please the eye as well as taste,
for those who die should be attractively
presented, otherwise their dish will spoil.

So gather rosebuds, do, clichés have use,
but keep their thorns from tearing tender flesh.

The Fool with His Coxcomb

If not for flaws, I'd lack distinction's marks,
as lacking qualities in finer arts,
those skills that lovers ply in poets' songs,
or painters' scenes of gently rendered nymphs

whose golden hues are focused by the light
that comes from admiration's silent gaze,
while those who look on beauty learn to see,
and not to see, so focused on its charm.

but I have not been shaped for sportive tricks,
no admiration's gazing meant for me,
so I must be content to play the role,
unhandsome though it is, of he that's left.

For I have often whispered my goodbyes,
and known the ones I loved did not love me.

Ozymandius in Miniature

We fill the world with images of self;
some in their work, while others use their art,
still others generation to express
the awful need for immortality

that cannot be denied, nor wished away,
nor reasoned with, as deathly shadows fall
between us and our every love, of life,
another's face, a voice expressing thoughts

we otherwise would be enraptured by,
except for dark and crushing pains that rise
from whence we do not know, unless from fear,
that master of us all, say what we will.

But images soon fade, and disappear,
and all our works, we mighty, cry despair.

Gods Among Us

Their mirrors hold them like a lover's gaze,
so full of passionate intensity
that other faces fade and disappear,
else merge into the one whose love they seek

and offer in return, for no one's heart
is so exquisite as their own, so fine
in feeling and in sensitivity,
so much a law of love unto themselves.

desire must be fed, and they will feed
at will on you, for what are you but food,
a momentary morsel for a god
who sees the world as naught but provender?

Their merest whims bring death to all they touch,
and your belief in them but whets the blade.

Olympians

With sudden clarity you realize
that you had been a prop in someone's show,
a stage device for his soliloquy,
or silent witness to her moving speech,

the men and women, gods who rule this world,
for whom the rest of us are but the foils
against which they stick fiery off indeed
in brilliance, privilege, and true beauty's form,

at least as measured in their own bright eyes,
still gazing in the mirrors of true love
and self-regard which has no need of you
except as furniture for empty rooms.

Such creatures recognize their own, though blind
to all the pain they cause mere mortal hearts.

The Sirens

Do not believe their words, deception's songs
that flatter passing sailors with the hope
of beauty that might one day be their own,
or understanding hearts that find a home

or something like a home, so one such said,
in those still fool enough to lend an ear,
a much too credent ear, to pleasing lies
that only lead to pain, and broken hearts,

in legendary tales of men transformed
to swine, or captured on an isle against
their will, amusing captives as they are,
to be cut loose upon the sea at dawn.

Their tongues deceive, and all their hollow words
lead but to death in kingdoms of the damned.

Canto XIII: In Solitude, We Cry

In solitude, we cry though no one hears,
perhaps take comfort in the swelling pains,
the ceaseless flow of urgent memories
still fresh, though details have grown dim with time.

too careless of our own emotions' cost,
we languish in our debtor's prison cells
without the thought of rescue or release,
strict wardens to ourselves with no parole

in sight; no rehabilitation serves
to render us acceptable to gods
or men, our sins forgiven, and our lives
refashioned after quiet, eyeless shades.

Still, who would want good names among the dead
whose Oleander leaves make mortal tea?

The Courtly Lover

My heart still stops each time I see your face,
I dream of you, of what it would be like
to hold you, feel your skin, and taste your lips,
then gaze into your eyes, and hear your voice
in cries and whispers through the heat of night,
to watch you paint the city lights and see
the world at twilight through your artist's eye.

I love the strength and courage of your soul,
the passion in your voice each time you speak
of art, and all the beauty you portray
each time you move, or smile, or lean your head
so waves of darkest silken hair reframe
your perfect face, and stop my heart again.

I'll never speak of this distress aloud,
so you'll not know, unless you catch my eye
at just the right unguarded time and place
a moment's slip, a much too rapid breath
whose rise and fall may give my secret voice,
and make me look the part of one who loves,
though I would always keep this secret close
and never see your face—despite the joy
it brings—before admitting to a love
I have no right to feel for such as you.

And yet, though I've no ground on which to stand,
no right to love you as I do, this fact
remains—my heart forgets its role, keeps still
where it should beat, each time I see your face.

Odysseus at the Mast

The siren song still calls my name at will,
as if it knows me for its dearest own,
my taste for darkness and its hidden truth
that all are as myself, imprisoned here

within the cages of our own design,
though mercy gifts the blind who will not see
the bars inside which all their lives are passed,
while mocking those who know themselves in chains.

For though I may be lashed unto the mast
and safe, for now, from notes that lead to death
in all its graceful melody unsung
for those who do not hear, I will return.

And having heard that wondrous song once more,
I will at last be faced with passion's cost.

The Harrowing

This western Pennsylvania mining town
had recently replaced its crossing guard
with one red light, which never seemed to switch
to green, as if to say, *abandon hope*

to all who entered there, as punishment
for sins committed in another life,
one lived exclusively in dreams, of course,
for no one thought beyond the bounds prescribed

by alcohol and services at church
where churlish priests refused expanded rites
to all Ophelias who escaped in death
without permission from a jealous God.

I knew one once, who managed to break free,
but at such cost as each must pay alone.

Motions and Pretense

It's just shit, you know,
all of this prattle posing as verse.
Take an old form—the sonnet—and wrench it
out of rhyme, or even any syntactical sense
and pawn it off as if it were profound,
but it's all too obvious what it is
and what it is not.

Christ, the fifth line in the "stanza" above
is perfect—if banal—iambic pentameter,
shit carved into form with the aid
of too much education and much too little talent.

Like the boy who used to pretend to throw fastballs
against the garage door back home,
the steady thud, thud, thud of the tennis ball
leaving dust circles on the dirty painted door...
the motions and pretense do not make
the thing pretended real, and tennis balls
will never be major league pitches,
just as a ceaseless flow of iambs
will never make poetry, no matter how much dust
they leave behind.

Thesis, Antithesis, Synthesis

The Cynic: People who are lied to deserve it. Those fools *want* to be lied to, *want* to believe the fairy tales the preacher tells them, the self-serving myths their parents taught them, the outright lies they themselves tell their own children.

The Optimist: Nonsense. Are all people merely liars and fools then? Are there no exceptions?

The Realist: There are exceptions, yes, and they are what makes life a tragedy, rather than a comedy.

Unto the Lord

Who makes a joyful noise unto the Lord
must first obtain a Lord. These don't come cheap,
although I have not priced one in a while.
The better models come with warranties

that guarantee repairs, and cover costs
of scheduled maintenance, since Lords break down
at inconvenient times, and rental Lords
are never what they seem in the brochures.

I almost leased one once, but changed my mind
on seeing contract limits to the miles—
Lords lose their resale value overused,
twelve thousand prayers a year, no more's allowed.

The public Lords can't take me straight to work,
so I will keep my Lord another year.

Soliloquy

We discover the truth in betrayals
of others at first, but next of ourselves,
we cheat, and marvel at getting away
again from the webs of our own deceit,
use words like "love" as sound effects that please
admiring ourselves in others' faces
gazing in their eyes to see reflected
the one face love returns us to each time
we venture out of doors in search of life
inside a world of possibilities
each new love adjunct to our own desires
each like the last, a mirror made of flesh.
I know you, who you are, or what perhaps;
a liar skilled, who passes for a man,
a woman fair, who lives without a heart
to pump the blood that does not flow except
in dust, from which you came, to which you'll go,
but not quite soon enough to save the souls
of those whose lives you'll touch, pretending love
while feeding that disdain that runs too deep
for most to see, the hatred you conceal
but not so well that others of your kind
are fooled or taken in by surface charms
as I can see the tricks you use to pass
among your prey unnoticed every night
still staring in reflective surfaces
for glimpses of your one true love, the one
who sees your shadow as you see yourself.

Jacob, of Rachel

Her hazel eyes pierce through pretension's veil;
their quiet gaze reveals you as you are,
laid bare before a living work of art
whose power yet transcends her beauty's form

while taking root inside the ones it sees,
where hearts become themselves, and growth transforms
the desiccated bud to fullest bloom
still turning toward her eyes like summer sun.

To live inside her eyes is space enough
for fairest show of who we'd learn to be
if only to remain in favor's sight
and stand before the altar as her priests.

This only is religion's use—to love
in wonder at the beauty of her eyes.

Immortality

I used to believe that I was immortal. But mine was not merely the immortality that all youth seems to believe itself the rightful inheritors of, no...mine was promised to me by the Brooklyn Heights priesthood of the Watchtower Bible and Tract Society, that quintessentially *American* religion in which salvation from death depends on one's *productivity*. Work hard, sell lots and lots of garishly-printed and poorly-written magazines, and most importantly...*never ever ask questions of any kind*...and maybe, just maybe, an ancient Mesopotamian deity with an anger-management problem will pass you by while he sets about destroying the entire world—old people, young people, children, infants, dogs, cats, and all.

To this day, death strikes me as absurd, an activity in which no one with any sense of style or taste would engage—I mean, *it's been done*. But we have no choice, apparently...and though my particular genetics in all likelihood give me something rather closer to a century than most, a century isn't really that much time is it? What is the damned point of dying? Yes, yes, the old story from Herodotus—count no man happy until his death, because we do not know the end of our stories until death...but is that all? Is that it? Death serves a goddamned *narrative function*?

And what of those of us so determinedly, even preternaturally superficial as to think that the fashions of this, or any other day are a reason to live in the face of something so absurd as death? Los Angeles is so full of such people it chokes on them a little more each day ... soon no breath will be possible any longer, so filled will this suburb in search of a city be with the legions of fashionistas for whom Anna Wintour (or Slavoj Žižek) is a power player equivalent to Machiavelli's Prince.

Perhaps it is—at least in part—due to such that Derrida referred to Death as a gift. But who wants such a gift? Perhaps we reach a point at which we all do. But not me...and not yet. And with angry gods to the left of us, and vapid Angelenos to the right, what are the rest of us to do but insist that neither theology nor thread count (theoretical or otherwise) gives meaning to life?

Oh well, screw us ... the latest issues of *Vogue* and *Critical Inquiry* are on shelves now!

A Christmas Poem

A king amidst the mindless and misled,
as seas of ignorance wash up on shores
where hordes of pointless rabble spend their lives.
These aren't the verses in a Christmas card,

as lacking merriment and odes to joy
and season's greetings standing in for love.
But would they were, for Christmas cards could use
some livelier revisions to their form

than common sentiments will yet allow.
So *Merry Christmas, Jesus hates your kids,*
or *Old Saint Nick would kill you if he could,*
or *Happy Hanukkah, Christ most hates you.*

Such cards would bring a warmth we often lack
on these, our special days of love's pretense.

Cloth Surrogate

My job has been to listen, so I always have.
A substitute in cloth, I don't feel pain or loss,
but I provide some comfort here to those that do.
I listen as they talk and tell me of their lives,
each inhalation preface to another tale.

I have no self to speak of, so I do not speak,
responding silently to others' needs and words.
None notice no one else is there. How could they know?
When listening to others is the perfect guise,
the perfect way to pass as if alive, as real,

without exposing twisted wire beneath the cloth,
the empty space inside that wires and cloth disguise.
I am not what I am, but not like him, the one
who wants to hurt. I help—at least I try to help—
though there is little that a surrogate can do.

But I can listen, while you talk and never see
I never talk about myself. Oh, I have jokes,
and carefully rehearsed details of others' lives
selected for similitude, to craft a life
eccentric in its color and its storied past.

But I have rarely needed my pre-scripted lines,
and not at all of late. My cloth and wires suffice.

The Other

Though I have fallen silent, drawn a veil
down over eyes that gave away too much,
my old companion manages my days,
allowing me to hide behind his face.

He's never failed me, since he first arrived
one day in pain when I could not respond,
he did, and since, has never lacked for words.
I do not know his name, though he knows mine,

knows everything about me, all I've learned
flows quickly off his tongue without my help,
no prompting or involvement now required
from me, no words remain he does not speak.

He saved my life, and now he lives the life
that I might yet have lived, if I were one.

Antigone in the Suburbs

With darkened light, her eyes still call to God,
while searching faces, whisp'ring silent prayers
of hope, imploring recognition's glance
from passers-by, though unaware and blind,

whose eyes give naught but darkness visible,
and cannot see her, neither what she was,
nor what she has become in loneliness
and silence, quiet depths where none approach.

She knows it fruitless, seeking in the dust
for love, or if not love, then intellect,
someone who sees, and seeing so sees her.
But still she searches, hoping to be wrong.

And as she searches, learns to see herself,
what once she was, and what is now, alone.

Trees

At odd moments I still remember trees,
especially one, whose roots would surface
as arms reaching up to hug or grasp me.
I always felt safe there, sitting with her,
the woman—girl really, barely twenty—
who loved me, telling me she was the one,
the only one who ever had or would.
I believed her, not knowing any better.
The scent of eucalyptus filled the air,
salt sea mixing with her and her perfume;
I could see only her, hear only her,
she told me then I was her little man.
I was only three, and would quickly learn
of love, of lies, of rage, of survival.

II
I could not stand her pain, nor hear her cries
without complicity or deference;
unless she were happy, even moments
of joy were dimmed and turned to waste and dust.
Soon I was set apart, denied contact
with the world, then even with those nearest,
who knew me as they knew a silent ghost.
That I was hers alone, not to be touched,
or even spoken to, lest wrath grow quick,
consuming all in flames of wounded ire,
they knew as if by instinct. Otherwise,
transgressions soon would be redressed in flesh.
I knew not why the endless silence palled;
nor nothing knew of other lives, unchained.

III

She told a story like no other could,
wrapped you in its rhythms, bought your belief
with widow's mite, while others treasures poured;
she needed to be loved at any price.
The lives of others were sufficient coin
to pay her debts of pain and loss and fear,
but always only for a moment's space
before the rage, expressed in calmest tones,
returned, announcing sure, for those who heard,
the other had revived, and sought its due.
But quick as it appeared it left again,
and she awoke, in tears lest I were gone.
In quiet and regret, she tended wounds,
while singing lullabies beneath the tree.

IV

With open book, she curled up on the couch,
while teaching me to read in my third year.
No primers served, nor ordinary books,
for she would soon lose interest and grow dark.
"The time has come to speak of many things,"
she read, of Walruses and Oysters then,
as through the looking glass we often went,
though soon enough returned, at least at first.
She was the former in the line, of course;
although I did not know what those words meant,
I learned their sounds and shapes, their rhythmic drive
and quick melodic interplays of breath.
An Oyster needs its shell to be secure,
though knives will soon enough lay all things bare.

V

Her father was a myth, a ghost, unreal
except in absences, where emptiness,
abandonment, and fear maintained their watch
before the high defenses she had raised.
Replacements proved their insufficiency
in later years; her marriages revived
her absent father, now in husbands' form.
The first refused her youthful ultimatum:
the band or me. He chose the band, and left.
The second stayed, but never quite gave in
to her demands, nor ceded his control
or choice of his career, his God, his life.
But he was absent too, for months at sea.
Her letters spoke of one who would not leave.

VI

The loneliness took root, grew wide and tall
with overhanging branches that gave shade.
Weeks and months went by in isolation,
no visitors, no reason to go out
most days, so filled with stories from her life
or books her fancy chose for me to learn,
strange tales of love and domination's cost,
the price that must be paid for loving men.
"You must not listen to the voice within,
because it lies—they love but to destroy;
and you must not believe as they believe,
behave as they behave, for they betray."
I did not understand then who she was,
but learned to see myself, and grew ashamed.

VII

To pare away all feeling left a core
as yet untouched, unreached and buried deep,
if not quite deep enough, for there she saw
the man, though still a boy, who would yet leave
despite his childish frame and quiet eyes
that only looked on her. She'd not abide
the thought that I might be like those she loathed
and worshipped all at once, though still expressed
in domination and submission's need,
in anger and in lust, in smoother words
than any could resist, or understand
in their true sense—incapable of truth.
No actor's talent could deceive that gaze,
and I had not yet learned my master craft.

VIII

"All men want only one thing; all women
exist to serve that need, say *yes, of course,*
comply, accommodate you fucking swine,
lie back and let you sweat and grunt and die.
Your scents disgust me, make me want to retch;
if only I could kill you all, I would.
But you will never disappoint, my son,
my only love, for you are not a man."
The other spoke this way, when she had left,
gone missing, lost behind the blue-grey eyes
iced over now with hate and rage and fear
of being left alone and waved away.
The other taught by hand, to prove her point,
and showed me what a swine a man could be.

IX

Concupiscence caused men to overheat,
inflamed with lusts they neither could nor would
control. What matter then, if heat caused pain,
she said, when ice could take that pain away?
Responding to her touch confirmed her hate,
proved I was but a man like all the rest,
though I was only three, then four, then five
as years went by and served their turn on me.
Each time was as the others—darkness fell
across her brows; the other soon appeared,
then took me by the neck to let me know
her will that I respond as if a man.
In aftertimes, she lay me down in ice
as if its melting water washed her sins.

X

And just as suddenly, what started stopped.
A creature of extremes, she would not touch
that too too sullied flesh that would not melt
nor thaw, nor yet resolve into a dew
as if in decorous pretense of health,
that all was well, that none required redress
for damage done, lest isolation bear
its will, defining all her future days
as acts of penitence and sore remorse.
no need, for life's next act came to our door
as paired evangelists, with God and Truth
tucked deep inside a leather satchel case.
So easily displaced was all her pain,
as absent fathers morphed to present gods.

XI (fin d'ete)

Revisiting my tree at summer's end,
what struck me was how small the setting was,
how near the street. Did I remember cars?
Were swingsets there, or monkeybars in sand?
The eucalyptus scent remains, the breeze
yet brings the ocean's salt, and children play
in sight of all, watched over by a few.
Such peace remains, when fires have burned and died.
We never spoke of early days again,
and when I left, returning for her death
alone, my sisters were the focus of
her eyes. Each knew imprisonment in time.
Though one recovered, one withdrew inside,
for both, I sit beneath the tree, and write.

From One Who Stands Outside

The door, I know, has not been shut to me,
it has been, rather, me who shut myself.
Though I have made a life of giving aid
to those who could not see illusion's masks,

of showing common lies for what they are,
distractions from the truth that sets all free,
I'll not go through the open door myself,
but stand in Pisgah's shadow, unredeemed.

Salvation comes to those who would be saved,
and though I know the way, I shun the path,
for mine is not a life that should be spared
but spent, so others less adept might live.

I am a secret hidden from the world,
and being told, I die, and am reborn.

Epilogue

Each sunset passes like the ones before
and I am one step closer to the end
of days spent waiting for...I know not what,
for nothings that I stretch to fill the hours

the no ones that I spend my evenings with;
what matter now the years of reading books
if all they ever brought was solitude,
long years of teaching those who do not read,

who hide their laughter with their folded hands,
the laughter aimed at me, and at the books
that I, a foolish man, would have them read
not knowing how pathetic I appear

to all the golden children for whom words
are nothing but impediments to life,
dull handicaps to love and sunlit days
soon followed by the gleaming silv'ry nights,

enjoyed by natural children of the world,
whose passions and desires are easily
returned by others like unto themselves,
while I sit with a book, and wait for sleep.

For I have been a fool who never fit
the vision of another person's life.

Exit

The time has come to pack away this life,
store tissue-wrapped regrets where none will know
the scars I've carved in those I leave behind,
as though my sins could find forgiveness here,

among the secret shames of youth and age,
and all the years between. What though remorse
may find new clarity, confessing all
the harms my life has caused, my breath inflicts

with passing of each moment I usurp?
Apologies ne'er mended broken hearts,
brought truth to those who fiercely cling to lies,
nor healed those broken by their misplaced trust.

Despite their weakness, these will be my last,
from this time forth, I never will speak word.

www.ingramcontent.com/pod-product-compliance
Lightning Source LLC
Chambersburg PA
CBHW020608030426
42337CB00013B/1266